Lost Inside

By Paul Moody

PHOTOGRAPHIC CREDITS

FRONT COVER: © RETNA PICTURES

© ALL ACTION

© LONDON FEATURES INTERNATIONAL LTD

© PICTORIAL PRESS

© REDFERNS

© RETNA PICTURES

Text © 1996 Paul Moody

Copyright © 1996 UFO MUSIC BOOKS LTD

For more information, write to:
UFO Music
18 Hanway Street
London W1P 9DD England
Telephone: 0171 66 181 Fax: 0171 66 078

The authors and publishers have made every effort to contact all copyright holders. Any
who for any reason have not been contacted are invited to write to the publishers so that a
full acknowledgment may be made in subsequent editions of this work.

Exclusive Distributors for the United States and Canada:

OMNIBUS PRESS
a Division of Music Sales Corporation
257 Park Avenue South, New York, NY 10010 USA

THIS EDITION PUBLISHED IN 1996 BY
UFO MUSIC BOOKS LTD, LONDON, ENGLAND.

Printed and bound in the United States of America
by Vicks Lithograph and Printing Corporation

oasis
Lost Inside
By Paul Moody

introduction
INNER CITY BLUES

TURN OFF

your mind, relax and float down stream to one bright Summer's day in the early eighties. At an all boys school in Burnage, South Manchester, a slight, crystal-eyed boy of sixteen, half terrified and half ecstatic at the prospect of leaving school, has three hours of his academic life to run. As he walks down the echoing corridors for the last time, it occurs to him that his life has already had its share of complications. At primary school he'd been the only boy allowed to wear long trousers due to a chill-inducing kidney complaint; at secondary school any bright sparks he'd shown had been swiftly diffused by a morale sapping dyslexia. Still, some things had felt right. He'd been born just as the Summer Of Love was coming into focus (on the day the Beatles announced the release of *'Sgt. Pepper'*) and he'd loved their music ever since he'd chanced upon the *'Red'* album as a six year old. But still. Here he was about to walk out of school for the last time without a single qualification to his name. Well, at least there was one score he could settle.

Seeing the loping figure of school bully Bartholomew Ganley ahead, he reaches into his pocket and pulls out the flour bomb he'd prepared earlier. Now, it seemed, was his chance to turn the tables for once - a tiny, irrepressible David about to slay his Goliath. As he throws the bag of flour however, his intended target dodges out of the way. Instead, it lands splat bang on the person behind him, who happens to be the headmaster.

"Congratulations' says the Head, minutes later in the musty confines of his office, before telling him that he won't be receiving his certificate of education today as planned. Instead, the school records will show that he was expelled.

Reeling from this last staggering turn of events the boy walks out of the school gates for the last time. As he walks home, heart pounding at the prospect of telling his parents the news, Noel Gallagher realises there's only one possible way to get his own back.

'I live my life for the stars that shine / People say it's just a waste of time / When they said I should just feed my head/ That to me was just a day in bed / I'll take my car and I'll drive real far / To where they're not concerned about the way we are / Cos in my mind my dreams are real / Are you concerned about the way I feel / Tonight I'm a Rock'n' Roll Star!' ●

*"Oasis star Noel Gallagher has told of the childh[ood]
which will come true when he steps out in front [of]
[40],000 fans at Manchester City's stadium on Su[nday]
[28]th. Tickets for the band's big 'thank you' to their [fans]
went on sale today with demand intense."*

Manchester Even[ing News]
Friday February [...]

BEFORE WE START, A MESSAGE FROM SECURITY: COULD ALL NON-OASIS FANS PLEASE LEAVE THE BUILDING...

HEN YOU come out of Manchester Piccadilly station the first thing you notice is the colour of the sky. High up to the left a lazy tangerine sun hangs suspended like a long lost maverick footballer, drifting through the clouds like a slow-witted opposition 'til it arches away, out of sight and off into the afternoon. Then you pull away, out of the station and to the left, and there they are, Oasis in poster form; those now familiar images plastered onto crumbling red-brick walls in larger than life grainy black and white. One has Liam leaning, as ever, into the microphone; hair a beautiful mop-top mess, shoulders back, lips curled around the mic as though he's bobbing for toffee-apples; and the other has Noel in that technicolour mod-chic shirt. Not saluting the crowd this time like on the Earls Court tickets but turning away to his left; those bumble-bee eyebrows furrowed in concentration whilst the crowd-who you can

only barely make out amidst the monochrome-gaze up in awe, waiting for him to release one of those atomic riffs, that'll make it happen, doesn't matter for how long. And at the foot of the poster, in huge letters, the precious words: *'TICKETS ON SALE TODAY!'*

Orange buses trundle by as the taxi heads down London Road until you see a small but perfectly formed *'Don't Look Back In Anger'* poster on a grey BT fuse box just like the one that'll crackle then blow up a few hours from now at the Piccadilly Box Office when the demand for tickets gets too great. Then we're at a roundabout, headed left, until we're temporarily caught in traffic behind a beautiful custard yellow vintage Ford being towed away to be revamped; and it reminds you that all the most beautiful things tend to come flying back at us through the past, retuned.

It turns right at the crossroads and soon we're speeding up, through green lights, past the University of Manchester and the Moss Side Sculpture Park and down Lloyd Street North, until slowly the excited girls at bus stops build up and then,

abruptly, there we are. A sharp left into Claremont Road, past the newsagents, the cafe, the City Chippy, and suddenly we're outside Maine Road.

Home to Manchester City, most days, but for today only it's became a mecca for something else, a teenage pilgrimage no less. Because everywhere you look there's young kids; hundreds of them in every shade of Oasis paraphernalia relishing the wait until the powers that be decide to open the box office and let them get hold of one of those priceless things; a ticket to see the band.

Some of them have even been here since two o'clock this morning, in the freezing cold, just to make sure they can get into the gig. And all talking about how much Noel and Liam mean to them, about how the records have changed their lives, about, well, everything. Christ, to them Oasis *are* everything. It's no more than three degrees in the shade this February morning, but no one here seems to care.

And the only thing you can think of, when you see the crowds, hear the softly sung chorus' of *'What's the Story'* and *'Wonderwall'* , or see younger, local kids ripping down the posters, plastered opposite in neat four-square rows, is how did Oasis get here? Twice as popular as any British group since the Beatles, three times as hedonistic and single-handedly responsible for re-electrifying the Frankenstein's monster of the British rock'n'roll group? The platinum selling albums, the Dom Perignon bath salts; even the chocolate coloured Rolls Royce - Oasis have got it all. But the question is *how much did they want it?* ◉

RIGHT, THATS THE POETIC INTRO OVER. NOW TIME FOR A QUICK THEORY...

HERE'S A question. What have all the truly great groups got in common? A lippy, heart-crushing singer? A phantom, dark-eyed guitarist? A secret, masonic teenage pact against the world? Well, yeah. But something else as well. And it doesn't matter how hard you stare into the photos, desperate to detect the answer. Because the one thing that all the great groups have got in common is that they always possess one member you'll never be able to see. You'll feel them sure enough; in the way the group are looking into the camera *just so*, or in the way a mediocre single might suddenly be saved by a chorus that fizzes around your head for weeks, but there'll always be there somewhere in the shadows, lurking just out of shot.

In days gone by these shakers and starmakers had names like Epstein or Loog Oldham, distanced from the chase for fame by class and a head for business, but in more recent times they could come from well, any age bracket or profession. Joe Moss gave the Smiths a fatherly head for heights; Gareth Evans, so it's whispered, was the one who conjured up all those wild ideas which set the Stone Roses up as demi-gods, fated never to play a gig when they could always stage a happening. But Oasis are different. Because the motivational force, the energy which propelled them from the darkest backwaters of Burnage to world fame is there every time you look at one of their pictures and see Noel Gallagher and those cool blue eyes staring from under that fringe right back at you. They got themselves a manager in Marcus Russell, just when they needed one, when they couldn't see straight for all the contracts flying around in front of them, but Noel had a more fundamental inspiration. He provided the drive to escape, the urge to wreak revenge for all the time he'd spent in other people's movies; tuning their guitars, making sure they shone in the limelight.

No more time in the wings those early photos seem to be saying; this time I'll be orchestrating things from the middle, right in front, lost inside.

GROWING UP IS HARD TO DO...

SO TOO bad it took so long to get things moving. Mr and Mrs Gallagher, first generation Irish catholics, had done their best to keep the young Noel's high flown aspirations on course. Mrs Gallagher spent her days at the local McVities factory picking mis-shaped Jaffa Cakes from the production line whilst keeping a watchful eye on the young Noel, whilst his father at least ensured some musical flavour filtered into the household.

A builder and part time D.J., he'd drag Noel with him on his travels around the local clubs until the prospect of another night listening to Abba's *'Dancing Queen'* segued into Charlie Pride's *'Crystal Chandeliers'* became too much to bear. But it was when Gallagher Snr allowed him to choose a guitar from the family's well thumbed John England catalogue that things really changed. Noel was thirteen and the black acoustic Gibson Hummingbird that arrived on the doorstep one morning looked like the most exciting

thing he'd ever seen. By then he'd already started getting in trouble. Experimenting with a lethal cocktail of Sex Pistols records and glue sniffing, he became so addled one day that he even broke into the local corner shop with a friend. The twitching curtains of Burnage did the rest.

Still, the six months he was grounded for as a result meant one thing. He could focus solely on the big-stringed guitar that lurked in the corner of his room. His interest was at best sporadic, though.

"Between the age of 13 and 17, I was completely out of fuckin' control" he confessed to Vox's Ann Scanlon. "I didn't give a shit".

Unsure of quite what to do next, he started getting acquainted, care of his father, with the local building sites. With brothers Paul and William (née Liam), Noel would spend the days being driven across Manchester in his father's yellow transit van, whilst at night he'd bash away at the

Hummingbird, playing the Animals *'House Of the Rising Sun'* and the Beatles *'Ticket To Ride'* till his fingers burned and his mum would be yelling from the bottom of the stairs 'til the windows rattled.

His parents split up pretty soon too, in his late teens, but by now Noel had graduated to working for a building firm sub-contracted to British Gas and had found his first real role model.

It was early evening one Thursday in 1984, and the Smiths first appearance on Top Of The Pops. The singer didn't make much sense, in a silk chemise and plastic pearls, but the guitarist was something else altogether. There Johnny Marr was, peering out from a thatched Keith Richards bowlcut and suggesting with every ripple of a chord, that the rights to cool were his and his alone. Noel,

suddenly realising that he too, with a little effort, could look this way, gazed at the screen dumbstruck, like a besotted Narcissus discovering his reflection. He couldn't get over it.

The days were still long, fruitless affairs though, and whilst dreaming one day a steel cap from a gas pipe fell onto his right foot, fracturing it badly. Once back near full fitness, Noel was given a less strenuous job in the store-room issuing wellington boots until the work picked up. After six gloriously idle weeks there, Noel realised that in stores things *never* picked up. He started to bring his guitar in and set about writing songs seriously.

Before any plans for world domination could be properly formulated, however, our hero became sidetracked. Chancing upon Clint Boon bootlegging a Stone Roses gig in 1989, the pair exchanged addresses and forged a friendship around their shared fascination. By now Clint had formed his own band, the **Inspiral Carpets**, and having been rejected as a prospective Inspirals vocalist (Noel had hollered his way through a Shaun Ryder-esque interpretation

of the Stones *'Gimme Shelter'*), he opted for second best. To his friends and former headmaster, Noel became the Inspirals guitar technician earning a princely £600 a week. To everyone else he became their roadie.

Striking up a friendship with future sound engineer Mark Coyle (then looking after the Inspirals' monitors) en route Noel became an almost Shakespearian figure. Often mistaken for Inspirals leader Clint on account of his bowl-cut hairdo(n't), he set about completing his apprenticeship as a musician under cover of the night. Whilst the band lounged in their hotel, eating grapes and telling journalists of the deeper meanings to be discovered in *'Sackville'*, Noel would go to work. He'd conduct soundchecks single-handedly, experiment with his own songs with Coyle on drums, and all the while watch the fickle machinations of the business like a hawk. As he explained to Q's Phil Sutcliffe:

"It was a great chance to sus it all out for three or four years. Being around managers, agents, record company people, journalists. I'd just sit there never saying a word to anyone going (the thinker: chin in hand, attention rapt)".

By now Noel was well aware of the hard toil that was interspersed with the thrill of the road. Too interested in drugs and high times to be really effective as a roadie, he nevertheless held on tight and travelled the world. America, Japan, Russia, Argentina; they all rushed by, as did the excesses which inevitably rolled along with them.

Noel didn't need telling twice. He'd eat cornflakes sprinkled with cocaine until his weight dropped to eight stone, at which point even his long-term girlfriend failed to recognise him. Suitably incognito, he started to take an interest in the girls who'd regularly follow the Inspirals backstage. *"Yeah, I've done all that groupie shit that the rest of them do now and believe you me, I had a fuckin' great time"* he later recalled to Lisa Verico in Vox ,*'I was as loud as our kid is. I did the same things he does every night".*

And all the while, fate was conspiring with him. Returning from the ardours of an American tour, he went along to see the progression of younger brother Liam's band Oasis (newly rechristened from 'Rain' in homage to the club at which the

Beatles had played their first Manchester gig) at the Boardwalk in Manchester in August 1991 supporting the long forgotten and, frankly, awful Sweet Jesus.

To an old hand such as Noel, the group seemed a half-baked affair. More a Sunday afternoon social club then anything else, they seemed to be mooching slowly down the road to nowhere. The songs were uninspired and Liam in particular, seemed to be saving up his creative talents for his days spent sabotaging the cars of Man United players at the local car valet service. But christ, he could sing. Noel, itching to find the right singer for his songs, saw stars.

"I told our kid the band was shite, but he definitely had something as a frontman. Then I said, you either let me write everything, control everything and make all the decisions or forget it"

If ever the four of them were to raise an objection it would be now; but they raised the white flag the minute Noel sat down and played them one of the songs he'd been saving up ever since those dusty afternoons in the storerooms. As he told *Q* magazine:

"I remember playing it ('Live Forever') to them on an acoustic guitar one night (sings) "Maybe, blah…" and it's one of the greatest moments I've ever had as a songwriter. They were just completely and utterly speechless. If I hadn't had the songs they'd probably have told me to fuck off!"

By October 19th 1991 the group were ready to play their first gig as a five piece, on a Tuesday night at a distinctly sceptical Manchester Boardwalk. Belligerent already (the band had put up a £40 entrance sign) the gig attracted forty people who saw them rattle through five songs. By now though, marshalled by Noel's ceaseless vision, Oasis had created a bubble around themselves:

"We'd go 'Fucking Happy Mondays, Stone Roses, they haven't got the tunes we've got".

For eighteen months the world wouldn't listen. What with The Roses off on

a quest for the holy grail (their second coming was still, it turned out, two years off) and Shaun Ryder rehabilitating in exile, the pop throne was clearly empty, gathering cobwebs with every passing week. And at the time a post-Stone Roses guitar band from Manchester seemed like the least attractive thing on earth.

The music press were in a tizzy too. Not a week went by without someone, somewhere, wringing their hands about the 'death of rock'n'roll'; whilst Suede - the great thin white hopes of the moment - flopped miserably in America whilst the dreadful Cranberries conquered all.

Worse still, homegrown groups - still sulking from having lent their dancing shoes to Dee-lite two years previously - were starting to believe the hype. It was all true, or so they believed. The fact was that prized rock'n'roll virtues such as arrogance and ignorance had gone the way of Birdland and they'd all better start looking and sounding like a pan-cultural musical jigsaw of the last thirty years.

And all the while Britpop was alive and well and living in a rehearsal room under the Boardwalk in Manchester. Masterminded with draconian efficiency by Noel, the group rehearsed ten of his songs, plus the Beatles *'I Am The Walrus'* solidly for twelve months. Encouraged, Noel forced an eight song demo onto a friend who's brother turned out to be Johnny Marr. Next thing the duo were exchanging notes on the joys of string-bending and embarking on a voyage to seek out new vintage guitar shops. This culminated with the pair getting on so famously that Johnny gave Noel his favoured white Les Paul (which had survived once belonging to the Who's Pete Townshend) and hinting that he'd pass the word on about the band. By April, Johnny's manager Marcus Russell had signed them up.

And by August, Alan McGee, full-time dreamer and head of Creation Records was in on the act. Stranded, so the legend has it, at Glasgow station, he decided to to make an early appearance at King Tut's Wah-Wah Hut where one of his own bands, 18 Wheeler, were playing with Manc hopefuls Sister Lovers. Aware that McGee was due to be present, Oasis strong-armed their way onto the bill through simple mathematics. If they weren't allowed to play, they reasoned, they'd simply smash the place up. Before a chord had been struck something appeared to be happening.

"I saw this lad in the bar" recalls Alan McGee: *"All dressed in white, really cool. He looked like Paul Weller".*

Nothing could prepare him for what came next however. A howling, shambolic mix-up of the Pistols and the stone-cold cool of the Stone Roses, Oasis simply blew McGee's mind.

"They were the band I'd been waiting ten years for" he later enthused to Select.

As the band came off he collared Noel and asked him if he had a record contract.

"To be quite honest, we'd have signed for anyone" remembered Noel to Q. *"But it was only Creation Records-Jesus & Mary Chain, Primal Scream, My Bloody Valentine. Give us it! I believe in fate and it was all mapped out"*

The wilderness period was now officially over. Having enthused wildly to Dave Massey, head of A&R at Sony America about the band, Massey duly came over to see them at the Powerhaus in London that November. Blown away, the deal was struck. Only, that is, after one more snag. On arrival at the Creation offices to sign the deal, Noel spotted a Farm poster on the wall. Unless it was removed, he explained, then there wouldn't be a deal. Get on, get on, that groovy train... ●

SJM CONCERTS presents

oasis + WHITEOUT

THURSDAY 24th MARCH 1994

DOORS 7:00pm

Tickets £6.00 (In Advance)

100 CLUB
100 OXFORD STREET
LONDON W1N 9FB
TEL:- 071 636 0933

00215

GOT ALL THAT? GOOD. NEXT STOP... THE LIMELIGHT!

CRYSTAL-BLUE cocaine stares, Armani braggodocio; drip-dry Afflecks Palace cool. These were the things Oasis dressed their dreams in. Installed in Monnow Valley studios in South Wales, the band released a one-off single called *'Columbia'* to the press in November 1993 and let the shock waves set in. Boosted by a chance meeting with Ian Brown in Monmouth, and revelling in the whispers surrounding *'Columbia'* (to date, their greatest cocaine fuelled fuzz-out), the band played a secret invitation-only London debut at the Splash club in January 1994 and promptly blow all expectations into orbit.

The press of course, were scurrying for their seventies colouring book as soon as the last thunderous chord fizzled out into the Kings Cross night air. Wasn't that a frozen T Rex riff just there? Weren't Oasis just a reworking of the no-nonsense thrills of Slade? Were Oasis just the Sex Pistols updated and then slowed down to thirty-three and a third? Definitely, maybe.

Caught brawling en route to a sold-out Amsterdam gig with astro-rockers Verve the band set out on a three week co-headlining tour with the persil clean Whiteout. Hotels got trashed, sceptics trooped home disappointed, and all the while the fevered whispers of greatness got louder, climaxing mid tour in predictably messy circumstances in front of a now besotted industry crowd at the 100 Club.

In the meantime the ever-fractious relationship between Noel and Liam exploded in a phosphorous glare in the group's first major NME interview. Already a fan, the NME's John Harris suddenly discovered himself, mid-interview, in the midst of a blazing burst of brotherly push'n'shove (later to be immortalised on Fierce Panda's *'Wibbling Rivalry'* single). The subtext was simply, the definition of rock'n'roll. But perhaps most telling of all the exchanges was Noels exasperated *"Oh fuck! That's it, man. Look, it's about MUSIC! MUSIC! MUSIC!'*

'Supersonic', released on April 11th, proved the point. Recorded and mixed in an eight hour session, it practically

redefined guitar music for the nineties in four raging minutes. First of all there was this howling, nails-down-the-blackboard slide of guitars and then BANG!, in its wake came a sludge of everything that had ever made guitar bands exciting in the first place. A black-hearted voyage into fast thrills, *'Supersonic'* was almost overwhelming, up there with the Smiths mesmirisingly self-absorbed *'Hand In Glove'* as a debut declaration of intent.

It was a simple equation after all, as Noel, ever the frank interviewee, was quick to explain:

"We're a cheap-shot band, just like the Beatles were. 'Supersonic' was a cheap-shot melody just like 'Hey Jude' was".

But lets slow down a little here. Because *'Supersonic'* was simply as cheap and nasty as great pop gets, made darker by an uncomprehensible lyric. Cue heavyweight reference: as Nik Cohn explains in *'Classic Rock'*,

great rock has always deliberately constructed its own language:

'and this wasn't just stupidity; it was a sort of teen code, almost a sign language, that would make (the) music incomprehensible to adults'.

Erm, got that?

The Beatles overpowering influence on Oasis' musical framework had been obvious ever since they first swaggered on stage and turned *'I Am The Walrus'* into a churning spasm of cocaine psychedelia, but here Oasis were nailing their colours to an altogether more self-interested state of mind. Full as it was of questions: *'You can have it all, but how much do you want it? You make me laugh, give me your autograph / Can I ride with you in your BMW?'* you just knew that no one involved was even remotely interested in the answers.

Footnote # 1: If anything the mood, encapsulated in the sulphurous burn-up of guitars and Liam's arsenic drawl was of a pure couldn't-give-a-fuck egotism. Much like the self-obsessed mood of the Sex Pistols' *'Anarchy In the UK'*, *'Supersonic'*

practically dared the listener to come a little closer.

Which came as something of an electric shock amid the brouhaha surrounding the nascent punk revival of the time. Like a light going out and a kick in the balls (or was it love or confusion, after all?) *'Supersonic'* rocketed straight into the top forty at thirty-one. Noel's dreams were suddenly beginning to have a tinge of 16mm realism seeping in at the edges.

By the end of the month the group were already back out on tour, interspersed with an abridged acoustic interlude at Creation's 'Undrugged' ten year celebrations and ever-increasing tales of the band's knack of grade A hotel trashing (Bonehead, it seemed, had finally found his vocation). On June 20th came *'Shakermaker'*. Already a staple of the live set, it was released in its original demo form (with a new vocal from Liam) and found the band still dripping in controversy. A jangle of Pink-Floyd psychedelia to begin with, it crawled shamelessly from the wreckage of the Beatles *'Flying'* whilst being a further victim of Noels way with an absurdist lyric.

Fearing a law-suit (pretty soon they'd be massing on the horizon), the opening line was altered from *'I'd like to buy the world a coke'*, to a more idiosyncratic *'I'd like to be somebody else'* but the theme remained. This was essentially a regression down the long and winding road to childhood.

The New Seekers lift was self-evident but the characters who populated *'Shakermaker'* had been hijacked from the late seventies too. So 'Mr Clean' jumped straight off the Jam's 'All Mod Cons', 'Mr Benn' from the drug-orientated animation of the time, Mr Soft from the 'Softmints' ad, and Mr Sifter less obviously, from the second hand record shop in Burnage where Noel had bought his first records.

Perhaps what was most powerful about the whole thing was it's audacity. After all, barely halfway through the song it practically came to a standstill, only to rally with a third verse of pure psychedelic whimsy:
'Mr Sifter sold me songs when I was sixteen / Now he stops at traffic lights but only when they're green' It was a request stop more or less. 'Come along, take a ride,

"If you're needing something I can give / I'll try and help you if I can"

jump aboard, don't be scared off by the mad, bad interviews. Shake along with me!'

Within a week the group had been banned from the Columbia hotel for their soon-to-be customary hotel wrecking (less of an achievement when it was discovered the only two previous bands to manage a ban had been the Fall and dreary goths the Mission). Having by general consensus stolen the show at Glastonbury, sandwiched between Echobelly and music press faves Credit To The Nation, and with

'Shakermaker' entering the charts at eleven, they then headed for the heathaze of the New Music Seminar in New York for their debut US performance. Here everything started to take shape. Coming on at midnight in the dripping Black Hole Of Calcutta conditions of Wetlands, the band blitzed their way past the rhetoric, harnessing, as the NME put it:

"The fury of the Sex Pistols with the sonic overload of Led Zeppelin".

Liam even wore a t-shirt bearing the legend 'Musician' (unproven, but the thought was there).

And the tours rolled on. A frenzied sell out trip around the UK; a hotel smashing spree in Sweden with Primal Scream which ended up with Liam jumping from the roof of a moving coach, breaking his right foot; they all came and went off. Still, the world just stood and stared.

HANG ON, AREN'T THINGS GOING A BIT FAST HERE? YEAH, BUT THATS THE POINT...

BY AUGUST it was time to release Noel's ace card, the bewitching *'Live Forever'*. A tribute to both Creation boss Alan McGee and John Lennon (the sepia tinted sleeve pictured the house in Menlove Avenue where John grew up), *'Live Forever'* simply had everything. The words alone were sheer poetry. From the opening: *'Maybe I don't really want to know / How your garden grows / I just want to fly'* the eternal Oasis message of living life as fast and as freely as is possible was established, but the song itself; built around a four chord sequence of G, D, A minor and C was as classically simple; pop songwriting at it's most succinct.

If *'Shakermaker'* had been a childhood kaleidoscope of pretty plastic images then *'Live Forever'* was the world turned dayglo and seen through the Hubble telescope.

Footnote # 2: What we're getting at is this. *'Live Forever'* was the sort of golden pop nugget the world hadn't seen since Shaun Ryder stumbled upon 'Step On' five years previously.

By now the whirlwind around Oasis was becoming uncontrollable. At Newcastle Riverside on August 9th a man assaulted Noel on stage after which three hundred people set about dismantling the band's tour bus.

Talking about *'Bring It Down'*, the song which apparently prompted the violence, Noel told the Melody Maker:

"It does incite violence. That song and 'Fade Away' are the two punk songs in the set, and it has kept getting hairy during those two songs. But I never thought it would come to somebody standing up on stage and giving me a black eye".

Regardless, *'Live Forever'* glided into the charts at ten.

Before there was a chance for a post-mortem the band were off again on their travels around Europe whilst debut album *'Definitely Maybe'* was released in the UK on August 30th. Having already been scrapped twice (once, famously when ex Sensational Alex Harvey Band member Dave Bachelor urged Noel to tone down the ear-splitting guitars) it arrived, third time around, as near perfect as a debut could be. ⬤

HMMM. BREATH-TAKING STUFF. BUT WHAT DID THE CRITICS MAKE OF ALL THIS...?

THE PRESS, giddy already from the speed of events, practically fainted. The central theme of the album, summed up by Select's Andrew Perry, was of life's possibilities:

"Everything is about Manchester dreaming- 'Slide Away's vision of escape, love and happiness, 'Up in the Sky' and 'Live Forever's glorious E-ed up rushes of invincibility".

Keith Cameron in the NME went one further announcing:

"With 'Definitely Maybe', Oasis have encapsulated the most triumphant feeling. It's like opening your bedroom curtains one morning and discovering that some fuckers built the Taj Mahal in your back garden and then filled it with your favourite flavour of Angel Delight. Yeah, that good".

Indeed there was something frantic and fantastic about the whole affair. Songwise there may have been few surprises (aside from the gorgeous *'Sad Song'* which graced the gatefold vinyl edition) but the quality of the songwriting was self-evident. Swamped in the

compression that Noel had been angling for all along, the record had the feel of early records by groups like the Who and the Kinks; who, eschewing any attempt at technical wizardry would simply let the guitar tracks overload, spilling distortion like a panacea over everything. But what Oasis added was a blue-collar earthiness unseen since Madchester.

Here was solid evidence that Oasis' improbable knack of blending store-room rock star fantasy, large dollops of acid psychedelia and overdriven production values were enough to shake the world. To its foundations.

Suddenly, as Noel put it:

"All the rumours, hearsay, gossip and sensationalism about drugs and fucking shagging in hotel rooms"

were just so much irrelevance. Oasis had taken the blueprint from the Stone Roses debut album and constructed something else altogether. On the precipice of the millennium, Oasis had opted out of post-modernism and constructed themselves a modus operandi around the bacchanalian pursuits of boozing, self-gratification and high living.

Following a six date UK mini-tour, remarkable mostly for the patronage of a past-his-sell-by date Lemonhead Evan Dando, the band decamped for a debut trip to Japan which sold out in two days. Shell-shocked from the ride Oasis found themselves reaching newly frazzled heights. Guigsy's eyes according to Daniela Soave in *GQ* were *'almost black and blue from over-partying'* but he still managed a Churchillian speech on the pleasures of the road, concluding:

"I can't stand these groups who whine on about how tough life on the road is', We love it and we go for it'.

Bonehead barely makes the penultimate gig. Even more tellingly, late at night in the hotel bar, perennial whipping boy Tony McCarroll receives a public dressing down from Liam: ***"You've got three weeks to prove yourself or you're out"*** is the parting shot. ⬤

QUESTION:
How could a band that was as frayed at the edges as this, still keep it all together?
ANSWER:
They couldn't.
That was August. Next would be September.

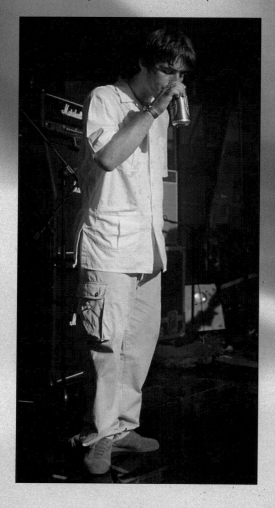

man, i had a dreadful flight!

"I was walking along and this chair came flying past me, then another, then another. I thought it's gonna be good tonight."

BEER AND LOATHING...

BY NOW even the simple things were starting to get complicated. Embarking on a five week trip to America, where home for the next fifty days would be a sweltering twelve berth bus, a twelve date UK tour was announced to keep the momentum going at home. It sold out in two weeks and the band released the anthemic *'Cigarettes & Alcohol'* in celebration on October 9th. A hedonist's anthem of the first order, it had a militancy about it that such party-singalongs usually lack. Yet the angst-free delivery (producer Owen Morris confessed to Melody Maker that the crackle and fuzz of distortion at the end of the track was only there because *"I was that drunk and stoned at the end I just put the tape on and stuck the faders up"* belied the content.

Because *'Cigarettes & Alcohol'* was, though cunningly disguised, a lament. The song came to the conclusion that *'Cigarettes & Alcohol'* were the answer to lifes puzzle, even though, as the lyric suggested, *'it's a crazy situation'*. The final exhortation, Liam's desperate sounding growl of *'Cos when it comes on top / You've got to make it happen!'* felt almost desperate; that, when there's nothing down for you, oblivion's the best route out. As such it contrasted sharply with, say the unabashed positivism of the Mondays *'Hallelujah'* or The Stone Roses *'One Love'*. Whatever, such psychiatrists' chair musings remained the stuff of anathema to Noel:

"We're a rock'n'roll band" he pointed out to the NME's Simon Williams, mid-tour. *"We say all you need is cigarettes and alcohol. Everyone's dead into analysing, but don't analyse our band. That's a good song that is. What does it mean? Who gives a fuck what it means?"*

Ironically, at the same time Noel confessed that the strain of perpetual touring had resulted in the break up of a six year relationship with his girlfriend in the Granada TV documentary 'With':

> # "I've lost a lot of friends. I've split up with my girlfriend who I was with for six years. I've lost that and I don't think I'll ever get over it'.

Like Alice's trip into Wonderland, things started to get curiouser and curiouser still. Their US tour was thrown into chaos following a disastrous gig at the Whiskey A Go Go in LA. Strung out from a seventy two hour booze-orgy, the group ended up going on stage with out-dated set lists and fell apart as a result. Predictably, a blazing row between Noel and Liam then ensued. An onlooking Ringo Starr couldn't tell the difference, being *'very impressed'*, but it all proved too much for the ever organised Noel. The end of the beginning had finally arrived, as he confessed to Paul Mathur at Melody Maker:

"I said to the others 'I don't want to do this if you're not going to put everything into it. Everyone just looked around and no one said anything so I thought fuck it, we're splitting up. I got $800 in cash that was the tour money and I got on the first plane out of LA. I had half an ounce of coke and I thought, "Right, I'm having this, then I'm going back to England. It's over".

Cancelling dates in Austin, Dallas, Kansas and Missouri, and with Noel now convinced the FBI were tapping his phone, he headed off on a one-man road trip through San Francisco via Las Vegas. This odyssey came to an end when he chanced upon, of all things, a music paper.

"On the way, though, I was reading through a copy of Melody Maker and, I know this is going to sound really sentimental, but I saw the advert for all these Oasis gigs in England and they were sold out" he told Paul Mathur, *"I didn't even know we were supposed to be playing half of them. We'd played loads of gigs in Britain, but this was the first big tour. I knew then I should go back to the others and we should sort it out".*

Marbles now relocated, Noel, ever humble, described the much talked about Christmas single *'Whatever'* as:

"The best thing I've ever written. When you hear it you can't get it out of your head. It's possibly one of the greatest songs ever".

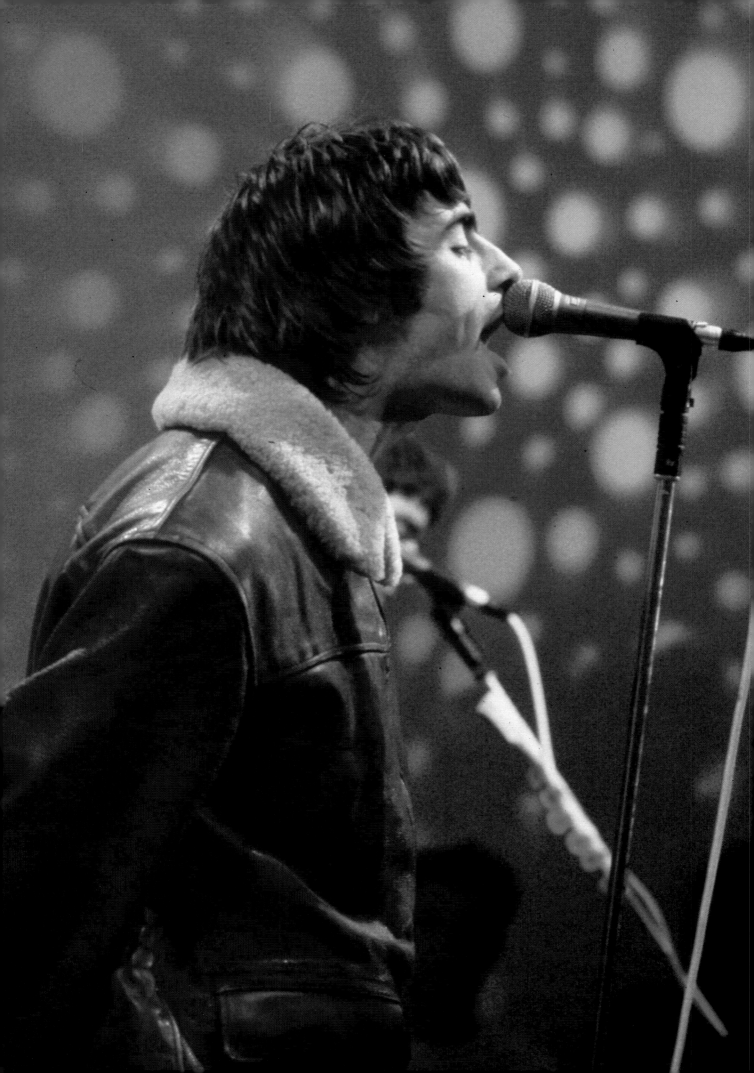

ALRIGHT, ALRIGHT. THEN WHAT HAPPENED?

BEFORE IT came out though, more legal problems emerged when David Bowie's lawyers suggested the band remove the *'All the Young Dudes'* coda from the record if they'd rather not see the Thin White Duke's lawyers across a courtroom. Plus more confusion ensued at a gig at Glasgow Barrowlands at the start of December. Liam, voice shot to pieces from the endless touring, walked off stage halfway through the gig leaving Noel to adlib his way through a further five songs. Rumours of a split still circulating, the band hastily re-arranged the dates whilst a rumour-hungry music press enthusiastically reported details of an incident in Paris the previous month where Liam had supposedly pissed in a hotel corridor. Like, whatever.

To celebrate news of *'Definitely Maybe'* going platinum, the band appeared on Jools Holland with a full string section to showcase their new magnum opus. Released on December 19th, *'Whatever'* marked a turning point in Noel Gallagher's songwriting. Ambiguous as ever, it was the first time Noel had been freed from the restraints of his own personal song mountain built up over the last ten years.

As a result, *'Whatever'* had a freshness and a vitality Oasis hadn't, up to now, possessed. Here was Noel in the first flush of success; unburdened from the need to load up on drugs and instead, contemplating all the things pop stardom should be able to afford him.

Footnote # 3: He was now *'Free to sing the blues if I want'* (a hint of the darker nature of the groups second album), but for now happy just to contemplate the prospect in the beat-centric fashion of Manfred Mann circa *'My Name Is Jack'*. Truly an exile from the Great Garbo home for wayward boys and girls.

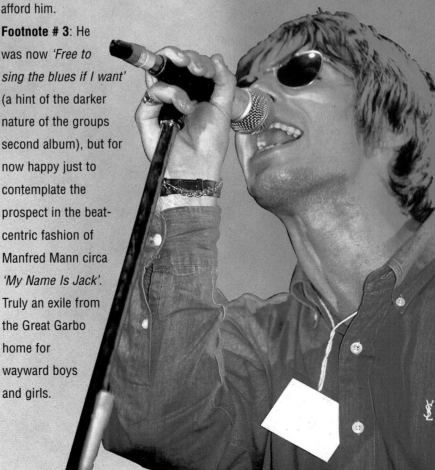

Liam in Damon impersonation shock!

DON'T TELL ME.
THE PRESS LOVED IT.
WELL OF COURSE THEY
DID...

THE NME SAW *'Whatever'* as something else altogether: as nothing less than a quantum leap forward. ***"A song to die for, with a descending scale and a fucking string section: from 'Love Me Do' to 'All You Need Is Love' in a year"*** enthused Steve Sutherland concluding, ***"these are the songs for the days we'll be nostalgic for in the next millennium"***.

Meanwhile Liam, bizarrely confessed that his drug of choice wasn't, as was widely suspected, cocaine, but erm, glue. As he confessed to a European magazine:

"I'm not into cocaine, I've got me glue me".

Even with a suicidal press campaign like this, *'Whatever'* sold 350,000 singles and only stalls at number five.

By January the news that the band would spend practically all of 1995 on tour coincided with Liam losing his voice, thus cancelling a debut visit to Australia. Having sold out a 12,000 capacity Sheffield show in April, the band flew out for a further gruelling two month tour of America. Before leaving, they collected all the silverware worth having at the annual NME Brat awards. At the industry sanctioned Brits however, they had to settle with Best Newcomers award whilst Blur swept the boards. Before the year was out, vengeance would be theirs.

By now America was beginning to get the point. With *'Live Forever'* climbing to the top of US radio charts, the general feeling was that Oasis, with their relentless touring, would succeed where all before them had failed. Their sound already had more in common with the turbo rock that swamped American radio, but, it was said, the group reminded people not of the fly-by-night attitude of Suede or Blur, but of the chaotic power of legends from a far off time called Led Zeppelin. News came through that *'Definitely Maybe'* had sold 220,000 in the US already and had gone into the US top 75. The suggestion was that by the time the tour ended the figure would have doubled. As if stunned by the prospect, Noel momentarily took his eye off the wheel and split his head open in a freak go-karting accident in Virginia. ●

A *'tired and emotional'* Oasis accept their 'Best Newcomer' award from a certain R. Davies at the Brits '95

ITCHING IN THE KITCHEN...

AND SO the waves of scandal and vice rolled on and the Oasis Titanic sailed on regardless. By March the band had returned to the UK halfway through their US tour and were holed up in Rockfield studios in Wales recording *'Some Might Say'*. Here the group hit more turbulent seas. Drummer Tony McCarroll finally received his marching orders in the wake of a bust up with Liam in Paris, and the news broke, typically, just as *'Some Might Say'* went straight into the charts at number one.

His replacement, forging ever-stronger links with the Paul Weller camp, was Alan White, brother of Steve (the Modfather's long term drummer). He then made his first appearance with the group the day after joining, on Top Of The Pops.

Amidst such confusion, it was easy to forget *'Some Might Say'* itself. Slight on first hearing, it became on repeated listening a rolling trashed-up marvel of a thing, drowning in more of Oasis'

characteristic wind tunnel reverb. The lyric, meanwhile, revolved around the life-affirming line *'Some day we'll find a brighter day'* as if one morning it might well wake up and find itself a self-respecting house anthem. By now it was becoming clear that Oasis' long held position as heirs to the Stone Roses crown had become redundant. **"They've one over on the Roses"** commented David Stubbs in Melody Maker, **"Who were always that bit too sullen and laid-back to reach the heights Oasis do here. Single of the year by a white hot streak, a moment in the sky we can all share"**.

Footnote # 4: It was *'Acquiesce'* however, which stole the attention. Hidden away on the B-side, it was the first acknowledgement from the warring Gallagher brothers that they might actually need one another. If anything the mood resembled that of the Beatles' *'Two Of Us'*, where a by then at loggerheads McCartney and Lennon realised the only way they could heal their differences was where it mattered, in song, man.

Meanwhile, sensing that their manic schedule would inevitably lead to a

**Opposite page:
Alan White, drum
saviour**

schism, Noel confessed his worries about the groups longevity to the NME.

"I don't see this going on forever" he announced to Ted Kessler. "I see it as three albums and that's it. I don't think I can do any more with Oasis after that. There's only so many anthems you can write".

Incredibly, by June he'd admitted that the band had already recorded ten songs for their second album at Rockfield, with plans to complete it straight after Glastonbury. A bashful Noel told an expectant *Q* that the world should be looking forward to *"a classic"*.

The band then played a warm up for the Sheffield arena show at Southend Pavilion. As their first UK gig of the year the press were, in the wake of the unbridled euphoria of the last twelve months, understandably cautious. The NME's Stuart

Bailie, sensing that the Oasis bandwagon was running wildly out of control, reported: *"You respect Noel for wanting to keep the band busy, to lash out those epochal EPs every few months, never dry up. But you also pick up signals from Southend that suggest his ambitions need to be reined in. Oasis need some recovery time".*

Just prior to Glastonbury and with the Summer already beginning to swelter into the hottest on record, Noel, playing peace-maker for once, confessed his respect for the likes of Blur and Pulp for keeping the standard of British pop high during the short spells Oasis weren't releasing records. Not that he was about to take anything as outlandish as a break. *"I'm not taking time off at the moment"* he told the NME. *"Not while I'm on a roll. Not while I'm making this much money. You see, I don't have the A-levels to fall back on".* ●

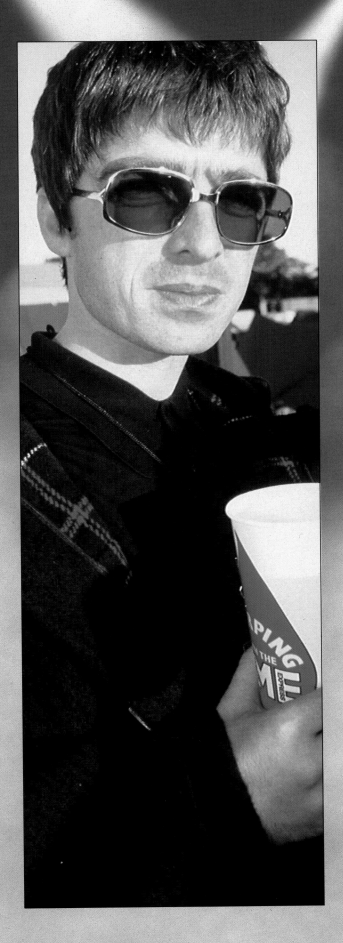

VERY NOEL. BUT WHAT ABOUT GLASTONBURY...?

THE FESTIVAL itself turned out to be a disappointment. Arriving hung-over from a long twenty four hours in Bath(during which they'd shot the sleeve for *'Roll With It'*), they became entangled with the press circus surrounding errant Take That member Robbie Williams. Consequently the expected triumph never materialised. Determined to redress the balance, they cancelled a prestige show with REM, and concentrated on applying the finishing touches to new album *'(What's The Story) Morning Glory?'* (a record, it transpired, only narrowly spared the title *'Flash In The Pan'*). Having completed the album on July 25th word soon spread about its quality. Producer Owen Morris claimed it was *'the best album of the decade, comparable only with 'Nevermind'.*

Amidst an absurd media campaign *'Roll With It'* was finally released head-to-head with *Blur's 'Country House'* at the height of the summer on August 14th.

On the face of it, *'Roll With It'* was yet another example of Oasis' knack of soldering a sure-fire melody to a lyric which encouraged an easy-going, almost passive outlook, but when you looked a little closer, it showed signs that the ceaseless touring was getting to the group.

When the chorus - titanic as it was - tailed off, what came in its wake felt like resignation; as if Liam was somehow singing a coded SOS to the world:
"I think I've got a feeling I've lost inside / I think I'm gonna take me away and hide/ I'm thinking things that I just can't abide".

Footnote # 5: The sound of the record was ragged too; apparently the result of Noel having turned up at the session after a heavy drinking session and collapsing under the mixing desk, only to be raised to record his part in one take. But this only concentrated the effect. Here was a sign that *'Roll With It'*, far from being yet another party-special, was in fact, Noel's *'Help'.*

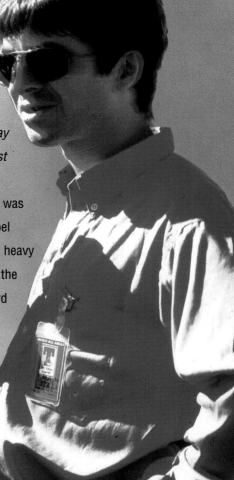

SO THEY WEREN'T SO SELF ASSURED? WELL YOU COULD PUT IT LIKE THAT...

ARK SUTHERLAND at the NME saw it as indicative of strain showing in the Oasis camp. Awarding Blur 'Single Of The Week' he suggested that Oasis' *"ludicrously overactive' campaign (was) 'finally taking a toll on Noel Gallagher's once seemingly bottomless well of crackin choons"*.

It was hard to argue. Oasis had driven themselves harder than anyone else in living memory, and the single showed it. Having flown back in from Japan, and frazzled by the failure of *'Roll With It'* to reach number one (something to do with a bar-code mix-up and the fact the Blur single was noticeably cheaper), Noel embarked on a forty eight hour bender with Paul Weller. Having arrived at the Top Of the Pops studios in the foulest of moods he registered his disapproval by making the band swap instruments for the performance, enlisting himself, in some dark reminder of his Inspirals audition, as singer. It looked awful.

Some amends were made when Noel stepped in at the last minute to contribute an acoustic *'Fade Away'* for the Bosnia album *'Help'* but as events were about to prove, charity, for once, needed to begin at home. The band announced a further UK tour only to have it cancelled at the eleventh hour with the news that Paul McGuigan simply wasn't up to it. The victim of nervous exhaustion, he was advised by Noel to *"eat more vegetables"* and the band quickly installed former Ya Ya's bassist Scott MacLeod as temporary cover on September 15th.

"We took his picture and we'll take his picture again at the end of the year." Noel announced gleefully to the NME: *"Do a before-and-after shot, see how much he ages"*.

Before the film was dry on the first one however, Scott's fifteen seconds were up. Within a month, and during a tour of the US and Canada tour, he announced whilst in Buffalo, New York State that he was homesick, and he left the band for a place in the Pete Best Memorial Museum immediately prior to a performance on the

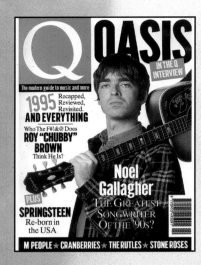

David Letterman Show. The band then blew out the remaining dates. But if this wasn't enough, *'Step Out'*. one of the proposed tracks for the forthcoming album was then deleted at the last moment owing to a startling similarity to Stevie Wonders *'Uptight'*. Meanwhile a second date at Earls Court was announced after the first one sold out completely in twenty-four hours. More controversy came when, talking about the album in mid-September Noel let slip to the Observer's Miranda Sawyer that Blur were less than bosom pals.

"The guitarist I've got a lot of time for. The drummer I've never met - I hear he's a nice guy. The bass player and the singer - I hope the pair of them catch AIDS and die, because I fucking hate them two"

Forced to apologise, the band made amends by paying a contribution to the Terence Higgins Trust. ●

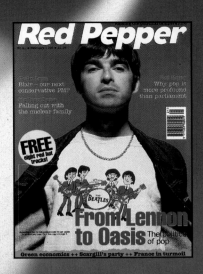

Liam trying out his musical skills on Bass at rehearsal whilst Guigsy has a rest

get no kicks from cocaine / I'm sure that if I took even one
iff it would bore me terrifically too."

Cole Porter
'I Get A Kick Out Of You'

IS THAT A BACKLASH I SEE BEFORE ME...?

SO ENDEMIC was the belief that Oasis had finally 'lost it' in the press at the close of the summer, that when *'(What's The Story) Morning Glory?'* finally saw the light of day no one could really be bothered to waste their time checking to see if it was any good or not. What with Blur's triumph in August and the increasingly candid portrayals in the press of Liam as some modern day working class lothario; a Lady Chatterley's Lover to titillate the tory-voting classes, Oasis' invincibility started to look like a mirage. Subsequently, much like the Stone Roses' absurdly undervalued *'Second Coming'*, *'Morning Glory?'* got short shrift when the reviews spilled forth, when time has proved it to be a classic.

A blind, solid-gold rush of sound, *'Morning Glory?'* showed that in twelve frantic months the tables had been well and truly turned. Gone was the aspirational drive that fuelled *'Definitely Maybe'*. Now Oasis were the rock stars they'd once sung about becoming. And everything about the album suggested they were hurtling toward some far-off destination they had no idea how to reach. *'Hey Now'* even spelt out this message of Oasis being star-struck travellers, blinded by success: *"I hitched a ride with my soul by the side of the road / Just as the sky turned black / I took a walk with my fame down memory lane / I never did find my way back"*.

The title track, probably the most anthemic moment the decade had yet produced, came, much like the Stone Roses epic *'Breaking Into Heaven'* from the darkest depths of the jungle. A cacophony of droning helicopters, and distant amp explosions, it simply screamed decadence.

Footnote # 6: Tripped out as it was, it was nothing in the blow-out stakes to final (swan) song *'Champagne Supernova'*. A modern-day 'Stairway To Heaven' if ever there was one, it found Noel sky high, where he'd wanted to be ever since *'Supersonic'*, but utterly lost at the same time. *"Where were you when we were getting high?"* was the question, but it was so full of resignation it almost sounded as if the party hadn't been worth throwing in the first place.

The production was even more overdriven than the last time round, but this darker mood was now something Noel was willing to expand upon. As he pointed out to Keith Cameron in the NME: ***"This is an album about what it's like to be in a group - which six days out of seven is a laugh, but half the songs on this album were written on the seventh day"***.

The critics, meanwhile, had a field day, and used the opportunity to pick holes in Oasis' limited range of influences like old women at a jumble sale. David Cavanagh at *Q* saw the album as proof of a group standing as still on record as they did live: ***"It baulks at most of the hurdles facing it, seemingly content to re-iterate certain basic points from 'Definitely Maybe'"*** he wrote, before ending, with an air of optimism: ***'It's unlikely that he (Noel) or the band have peaked; one erratic flight cannot blow up all four engines, but now it's time for a musical rethink"***.

Whilst the punditry rages, it sold 350,000 copies in the first week.

Short on options, and with two enormous shows at Earls Court approaching,

a frail Guigsy was ordered to report for bass duties under threat of expulsion. The gigs, subsequently, as well as being the biggest indoor shows ever staged in Europe, vindicated the album completely. The mood each night, a heady cocktail of drunkenness and euphoria, was if anything, beyond triumphalist. Here, finally, was proof of the group's pole position in the pop hierarchy.

Having spent nearly half the year out of the country, Oasis, over two nights, had fearlessly performed the feeding of the forty thousand. To invoke Shaun Ryder, they evidently had balls bigger than King Kong.

**Oasis invade
Earls Court,
November '95**

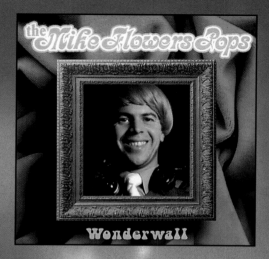

In any case, the occasion was quickly eclipsed by the release of the marvellous *'Wonderwall'* as a single and, in quick fire-succession, the Christmas success of Mike Flowers' hastily prepared cover version. Easy listening schmaltz as it was, it still provided the perfect setting for Noel's eternal aspiration to be taken seriously as a songwriter. After all,

Bacharach fan as he was, Noel had previously arranged his songs as if they were recorded in a wind tunnel on the world's largest amplifiers.

Footnote # 7: Cleansed of the distortion and the dripped-sarcasm vocal of his younger brother, *'Wonderwall'* became pop par excellence, and was only denied a deserved number one by Michael Jackson's dreary *'Earth Song'*.

The net result was that the band's own version of

'Wonderwall' found itself soaring back up the charts. So indecently, in fact, that follow up 'Don't Look Back In Anger' (released on February 19th), had to be delayed until it finally ran out of steam. The song itself was described by Paul Weller, no less, as *'the best song of the nineties'*. What it heralded, however, was slightly less subjective. Having already stormed the Brat Awards, and, more significantly, the Brits, winning everything worth winning at both, the record then entered the charts at number one.

With 'What's The Story' still in the US top five and 'Wonderwall' number one in Australia, the world went Oasis mad. Accordingly, Burnage was officially declared centre of the universe, a fifty foot cast iron statue of Liam erected in Piccadilly Square and the Brothers Gallagher awarded the keys to Buckingham Palace. Well, metaphorically at least.

All of which brings us up to date. But wait! There's still time for a final page conclusion...

Newsflash: Noel's mantlepiece reinforced after NME Brat Awards

Liam, meanwhile, waxes lyrical at the Brits about his newly discovered allergy to shaving foam

SINGLES

Columbia *(demo)*
Creation CTP 8
(12" one-sided promo only)
December 1993.

11TH APRIL 1994
Supersonic
Take Me Away
7" Creation CRE 176

Supersonic
Take Me Away/ I Will Believe (Live)
12" Creation CRE 176T

Supersonic
Take Me Away / I Will Believe (Live)
Columbia (Demo)
CD Creation CRE 176

20TH JUNE 1994
Shakermaker
D'Yer Wanna Be A Spaceman
7" Creation CRE 182

Shakermaker
D'Yer Wanna Be A Spaceman
Alive (8 track demo)
12" Creation CRE 182T

Shakermaker
D'Yer Wanna Be A Spaceman
Alive (8 track demo)
Bring It On Down (Live)
CD Creation CRESCD 182

8TH AUGUST 1994
Live Forever
Up In The Sky (acoustic)
7" Creation CRE 185

Live Forever
Up In The Sky (acoustic) / Cloudburst
12" Creation CRE 185T

Live Forever
Up In The Sky (acoustic) / Cloudburst
Supersonic (live)
CD Creation CRESCD 185

OCTOBER 1994
I Am The Walrus (live)
Promo 12"
Creation CTP 190

9TH OCTOBER 1994
Cigarettes And Alcohol
Promo 12"
Creation CRE 195TP

Cigarettes And Alcohol
I Am The Walrus (ive)
7" Creation CRE 190

Cigarettes And Alcohol
I Am The Walrus (live)
Fade Away
12" Creation CRE 190T

Cigarettes And Alcohol
I Am The Walrus (live)
Listen Up / Fade Away
CD Creation CRESCD 190

DECEMBER 1994
Whatever
Promo one-sided 12"
Creation CRE 195TP

(It's Good) To Be Free
Promo one-sided 7"
Creation CTP 195

19TH DECEMBER 1994
Whatever
(It's Good) To Be Free
7" Creation CRE 195

Whatever
(It's Good) To Be Free / Slide Away
12" Creation CRE 195T

Whatever
(It's Good) To Be Free
Half THe World Away/ Slide Away
CD Creation CRESCD 195

4TH MARCH 1995
Some Might Say
Talk Tonight
7" Creation CRE 204

Some Might Say
Talk Tonight / Acquiesce
12" Creation CRE 204T

Some Might Say
Talk Tonight / Acquiesce / Headshrinker
CD Creation CRESCD 204

4th August 1995
Roll With It
It's Better People
7" CD Creation CRE 208

Roll With It
It's Better People / Rockin' Chair
12" Creation CRE 208T

Roll With It
It's Better People / Rockin' Chair
Live Forever (live)
CD Creation CRESCD 208

30th October 1995
Wonderwall
Round Are Way
7" Creation CRE 216

Wonderwall
Round Are Way / The Swamp Song
12" Creation CRE 216T

Wonderwall
Round Are Way / The Swamp Song
The Masterplan
CD Creation CRESCD 216

19TH FEBRUARY 1996
Don't Look Back In Anger
Step Out
7" Creation CRE 221

Don't Look Back In Anger
Step Out / Underneath The Sky
12" Creation CRE 221T

Don't Look Back In Anger
Step Out / Underneath The Sky
Cum On Feel The Noize
CD Creation CRESCD 221

ALBUMS

30TH AUGUST 1994
DEFINITELY MAYBE
CD Creation CRED CD 169
Rock'n'Roll Star / Shakermaker
Live Forever / Up In The Sky / Columbia
Supersonic / Bring It On Down
Cigarettes And Alcohol / Digsy's Dinner
Slide Away / Married With Children
also available on double album vinyl
(CRE LP 169)
includes extra track *Sad Song*.

2ND OCTOBER 1995
(What's The Story) MORNING GLORY?
CD Creation CRED CD 189
Hello / Roll With It / Wonderwall
Don't Look Back In Anger / Hey Now!
Some Might Say / Cast No Shadow
She's Electric / Morning Glory
Champagne Supernova
also available on double album vinyl
(CRE LP 189) includes extra track
Boneheads Bank Holiday

INNER CITY BLUES

PERHAPS THE PHENOMENAL SUCCESS OF OASIS can be attributed to something other than Noel Gallagher's drop-dead classic songwriting, Liam's sandpaper-dry drawl of a vocal and the cartoon image of the group as being a Mancunion *Spinal Tap*, determined to have a good time all the time. But I doubt it. Had the Stone Roses returned with an album as instantly accessible as *'Definitely Maybe'* rather than the wonderful, if ponderous *'Second Coming'*, things may have been different; the debt Oasis owe to the Roses, is, after all, the size of Bolivia's national debt. The thing to remember though, is that for all the self-aggrandising rhetoric, Noel Gallagher has single-handedly made rock music popular again. He's a beautiful dreamer disguised in Levis; a poet in Paul Smith, and we shouldn't forget it. So what if Oasis' songs have all the innovative drive of the Luddites; rocking shamelessly all over the world. 'Quoasis' always had a ring to it.

The point is they've banished forever the notion of rock'n'roll sounding like an outdated concept; like the noise coming out of a bedroom that pop wasn't interested in anymore. And impressively, despite number one records all around the world, Noel Gallagher appears to be under no illusions of the task ahead, as he explained recently to Laura Lee Davies in Time Out:

"We're not a big group really. Until I get into a black cab and the drivers constantly know who I am, I'll consider us an average, run-of-the-mill group. Until I get in a cab in New York and the driver says, "Hey, Oasis!", then, compared to U2, we're just tiny kids rolling tyres around".

What he appears to be forgetting, of course, is that he's practically there already.

TAXI!!!!!